-------- WHAT (

"Jamie Levy has done it again. As in his previous book "Philanthropy," Jamie provides us with an easy-to-follow guide to a large and complex topic. Jamie's deep understanding and experience of philanthropy has allowed him to get straight at what matters most to the men and women who serve our causes as board members. If your board needs a tune-up, this is the book for you."

— RICHARD KLOPP
CEO, Water for Good

"Philanthropy comes in many forms and with many definitions. But its Greek origin, the love of mankind, is often overlooked in favor of the trendy language of the day, often missing the point: that this is about people, relationships and a passion to serve. Jamie Levy has managed to bring the governance principles and practices of well-done philanthropy to life in such a way that it connects the people with the purpose. Whether a veteran board member or a first-timer to this crucial role of governance, this book provides the answers to the most fundamental questions of board leadership and potential. Its lessons are embedded in a skillful portrayal and clarity of the independent sector that exists solely to serve others with passion and competence. It will be a "go to" reference that everyone keeps handy in their work."

— MASON B. RUMMEL
President & CEO, James Graham Brown Foundation

WHAT OTHERS ARE SAYING

"Jamie Levy helps give the specifics of how a board member can help lead. No stone is left unturned in detailing the roles and responsibilities for board members. Read this and you will have all the tools necessary to be a world-class board member."

— JAY HEIGHT
Executive Director, Shepherd Community Center, Indianapolis

"Behind every flourishing nonprofit is a strong, supportive board. However, many board members find themselves unaware of the key responsibilities they are charged with. This book equips both board members and Executive Directors with detailed instructions to help board members, boards, and organizations thrive."

— GINA GIBSON
Executive Director/CEO, Evansville Christian Life Center

I'M A BOARD MEMBER. *NOW WHAT?*

?

DISCOVER YOUR NONPROFIT BOARD'S TRUE POTENTIAL

JAMIE LEVY

ISBN-13: 978-1-7336375-1-0 (JDLevy & Associates)

JDLevy & Associates, Inc.
PMB 102
3557 N. Newton Street
Jasper, IN 47546

jdlevyassociates.com

In our years of work teaching, consulting, and studying the nonprofit sector, and through the work of numerous others in the field, it is apparent that the greatest factor in the future sustainability of a nonprofit organization is the strength and health of its board.

The board often sets the growth ceiling of the nonprofit organization. The concepts in this book can help build, grow, and sustain your board, organization, and therefore the cause you are working for.

I want to extend a deep thanks to the many boards and leaders I have been privileged to work with who are leading the way to making a better society. As you reflect through this book, I encourage you to remember that serving on a board is a true privilege of service.

Thank you,

Jamie D. Levy
Jeremiah 33:3

CONTENTS

SECTION I

OVERVIEW

CHAPTER 1

PHILANTHROPY AND THE BOARD

Philanthropy simply means love of man and woman kind.

What is philanthropy?

If you ask the average person, you'll get answers ranging from a new form of financial investment to the study of some guy named Phil. In all seriousness, philanthropy is a term that is critical to our society but often not understood.

Philanthropy simply means love of man- and woman-kind. It refers to spirit or action for the good of human-kind. Philanthropy is expressed through giving of money and material, volunteering for a cause we believe in, and through advocacy for our passions and values.

Nonprofit organizations are primary means for the expression of philanthropy—they exist to meet societal needs and engage people in a cause close to their heart. Philanthropy represents an exchange of values and social relationship. It provides value for both giver and receiver. The receiver gets their need met and the giver expresses their values by participating in a cause they believe in.

Philanthropy occupies a different part of the economy from business or government. You may be surprised by the potential for influence the charitable sector has:

- *The charitable sector includes nearly 1.6 million tax-exempt (nonprofit) organizations.* [1]
- *Charitable sector revenue includes nearly $1.4 trillion.* [1]
- *The charitable sector's share of Gross Domestic Product is 2.1%.* [2]
- *Nonprofits account for 10% of all wages and salaries paid in the United States.* [3]
- *Nonprofit volunteers provide more than 8 billion hours of service time, creating more than $193 billion in economic value.* [4]

?

The board of a nonprofit organization is the heart of an organization structured to serve through philanthropy. As a body of servants designated and designed to lead an organization in serving the public good, the board is one of the single most important elements in the sustainability of a nonprofit organization. A board's actions will make or break the future of that organization. The board defines the growth ceiling of the organization, either contributing to its development or allowing for its stagnation.

Today's board is often diminished, viewed only as a group of people attending meetings, rather than a body of leaders designed to serve and change lives. As a result, the average board seems to have reduced its members from passionate champions for a cause to mere commodities. Modern boards are often not formed from passion, but from those who bring the greatest image, experience, stature, or wealth to the table. Passion for the cause takes a backseat and can lead to dysfunction at the board level.

Rather than being extolled by the organization as lifelong leaders, the board and its members have been degraded. A short-term mindset has replaced the notion that these leaders should be valued as lifelong relationships to the organization, as advocates who will go far beyond their duty of board serving.

Building a board able to maintain a generationally-sustainable organization requires a proper definition and understanding of philanthropy. The board is not about itself or its members; it is about philanthropy, the good of society. The board is to become a body of leadership centered on its synergized passion and collective wisdom—accepting responsibility and rejecting passivity. Boards become transcendent when they are galvanized to champion and advocate a cause that is changing lives and strengthening civil society.

?

CHAPTER 2

THE NONPROFIT BOARD TODAY

The board is the single most important body of any nonprofit organization.

Board of Directors. Regents. Trustees. Overseers. Governors. The Board. All these names refer to the governing body of a nonprofit organization. For religious organizations, the board may even take other names, such as vestries, leadership team, or elders.

No matter what name it goes by, the board is the single most important body of any nonprofit organization. Not only is the board legally responsible for the organization, but its members are also socially responsible for being good stewards of the organization's resources. They ensure the organization's mission is fulfilled and that the organization is a dependable and effective steward of the resources entrusted to it by donors.

The highest purpose of a nonprofit organization is to act for the good of the community served by the organization. In other words, it is the board's responsibility to safeguard the public good. To accomplish this, a board must be comprised of committed individuals who fully understand their roles and obligations and share a common passion for the cause. Furthermore, all board members must function together as a cohesive unit, a body of leadership that serves, and thereby governs, the organization towards the achievement of its mission.

By law, the board and its members are held accountable for the actions and inactions of the organization. To help establish accountability, a board and its members should continually evaluate its mission, stewardship, and leadership results.

In short, a board is a huge factor in determining the ultimate success or failure of an organization. As a board member or potential board member, the most important thing you can do is to define and understand your duties and responsibilities.

I liken the board to the example of the NBA and its early years involved with the Olympics. Early on, the great NBA players went to the Olympics. They performed as a group of great individual players but not as a team and, as a result, they did not do very well. It was not until that group of players became a team that they became great. Boards are very similar. Unless we move from a board of individual directors to a true body or team of leadership, the full potential of any organization will be underachieved.

The importance of the board was established during the formalization of the not-for-profit sector. In the first legal step towards legally recognizing the not-for-profit sector, the Revenue Act of 1894 established incentives to have defined, formal volunteer boards with tax-exempt status for nonprofits. Later, the Revenue Act of 1954 established Section 501c (3) of the Internal Revenue Code, the designation for a tax-exempt charitable organization, which set forth certain responsibilities for board members.

Following this, we saw the further procurement of the board in the Not-for-Profit Organization Act of 1971. This act defined the board as the core group of individuals, three in some states, who were responsible for the organization and set forth formal guidelines for not-for-profit boards.

Not-for-profits serve society in the form of charities, foundations, social welfare, professional, and trade organizations in twenty-eight different classifications. Ranging from cemeteries, to trusts, to service providers they serve in areas that neither government nor business can do as effectively. As of 2013, there were 1.4 million registered nonprofit organizations in the U.S., and almost 1 million of those are registered 501(c)(3) public charities[1]. In the past, Americans gave

$410 billion to charities[2] and about 25 percent acted as a volunteer[3]. The sector is diverse, pioneering, adventuresome, and exciting. Despite the great variations in those organizations that serve, they all have one thing in common: every nonprofit organization, by law, is governed by a board of directors.

ACTIONS:

Compile and review historical information about your organization and board.

Seek to understand how the board has historically functioned, how it demonstrates accountability, and how it moves the organization toward fulfillment of the mission.

CHAPTER 3

TAX-EXEMPT STATUS AND ITS IMPLICATIONS

Not understanding the parameters of activity could result in consequences that threaten an organization's tax-exempt status.

The tax-exempt status of nonprofit organizations causes boards to have increased responsibility as it reinforces the public good and trust. It is the board's responsibility to understand the 28 different classifications of nonprofits under the IRS Code. Not understanding the parameters of activity could result in consequences that threaten an organization's tax-exempt status.

The differences under these classifications range from the tax deductibility of donations to limitations on lobbying government. The typical not-for-profit organization, the charitable not-for-profit, falls under section 501(c) 3 of the IRS Not-for-Profit code. Contributions made to 501(c) 3 organizations are tax deductible.

It is highly recommended all new board members understand the purpose and classification of their organization so they, along with the full board, can prevent actions that may result in the loss of the tax-exempt status of the organization.

ACTIONS:

Research and understand the purpose and classification of your organization.

Consult the organization's bylaws, articles of incorporation, Section 501(c)3 of the IRS Not-for-Profit code and any other documents referring to your board's tax status.

SECTION II

BOARD GOVERNANCE AND OPERATIONS

CHAPTER 4

LEGAL DUTIES OF THE BOARD

As a board member, you are legally obliged to meet certain standards of conduct.

Do you know your legal duties as a board member? As a board member, you are legally obliged to meet certain standards of conduct, known as Duty of Care, Duty of Loyalty, and Duty of Obedience. Often, and mistakenly, a board's legal duties take a backseat to other pressing issues. Board members, however, must always be aware of, and responsive to, their legal obligations.

Duty of Care.

The Duty of Care charges the board and its members with the obligation to act in good faith and carry out its activities with the care that an ordinarily prudent person would exercise under similar circumstances, while protecting the organization's assets (money, property, goodwill, people, integrity). This also includes being diligent, attending meetings, and becoming acquainted with the issues prior to forming a decision that involves the organization or is made on behalf of the organization.

Duty of Loyalty.

The Duty of Loyalty calls for allegiance and faithfulness to the organization. Every board member must act according to the best interest of the organization and must not place his or her personal interests above the interests of the organization.

Duty of Obedience.

The Duty of Obedience dictates that board members shall act lawfully, in respect of and in accordance with the organization's mission, charter, and donors' intent.

Remember, board members are stewards of publicly entrusted money and need to be aware of their obligations, which require board members to act diligently, attend board meetings, stay informed, act according to the best interest of the organization, follow the organization's mission and charter, and obey donor intent.

It is much easier to uphold these mandates if you care about the organization's cause. For example, if your organization saves lady bugs, a board member who doesn't really care about lady bugs might find it difficult to uphold these IRS mandates of service.

?

ACTIONS:

Discuss with your fellow board members the three duties outlined above.

What do these duties mean specifically for you and your organization?

CHAPTER 5

BOARD RESPONSIBILITIES

A nonprofit board is responsible for the organization, its finances, relationship with the community, and legal requirements.

Beyond the three legal duties, what are the board's roles and responsibilities? This question is often asked yet seldom fully answered. Too often board members are not aware of the full scope of the board's responsibilities and therefore risk breaching public trust, failing its mission and the community it serves. Having a complete understanding of its basic responsibilities is critical to the success of any nonprofit board.

In summary, a nonprofit board is responsible for the organization, its finances, relationship with the community, and legal requirements.

Responsibility for the Organization

To carry out responsibility for the organization, a board of directors:

- ***Shapes the organization's mission and vision***
  - *Shares a common understanding of the mission and vision*
  - *Defines, periodically refines, and sustains the organization's purpose*
  - *Develops and implements policies that fulfill its objectives*
  - *Reviews policies and strategies to ensure their effectiveness and adherence to the proper end*
  - *Ensures programs and services adhere to the mission's aim*

- ***Undertakes strategic planning and policy decisions***
  - *Employs a planning process that fosters joint board and staff ownership and operates within the context of changes to the external environment*
  - *Constructs a plan for the long-term growth that is tightly linked to the mission and vision*
  - *Distinguishes between board and management-level decisions*

- ***Selects, hires, supports, evaluates, co-leads with and, if necessary, terminates the CEO or Executive Director (ED)***
  - *Plans for succession of the CEO or ED*
  - *Evaluates and communicates CEO or ED performance annually*

- ***Identifies, secures, and stewards adequate financial resources to fulfill the stated mission***
  - *Determines strategic funding priorities and needs*
  - *Gives individually to support the organization*
  - *Participates in fundraising planning*
  - *Helps secure financial resources from the community*

- ***Provides influence, expertise, and experience***
  - *Identifies access and influence needs based on strategic goals and proactively fulfills those needs*
  - *Identifies expertise and experience needed to meet strategic goals and acts to obtain those skills*
  - *Aids in discerning and directing organization's landscape*

?

- ***Monitors and periodically evaluates the organization to ensure accountability***
  - *Works with staff to evaluate program and mission alignment*
  - *Sets regular evaluation periods and uses results to improve strategy and resource allocation*
  - *Obtains feedback and open communication with stakeholders*

- ***Safeguards the organization through written policies and best practices***
  - *Develops a written code of ethics, whistleblower protection policies, document retention policies, and decision-making policies*

- ***Translates theoretical strategy into reasonable goals for the board***

- ***Regularly assesses its performance against these aims***

- ***Evaluates individual director performance; provides developmental assistance as needed***

- ***Improves its own performance***

?

Responsibility for the Organization's Financial Performance

To carry out responsibility for the organization's financial performance, a board of directors:

- *Prepares and reviews financial plans in context of the strategic plan and mission*
- *Monitors financial statements and investment performance; communicates with staff, if needed*
- *Ensures timely, independent audit of financial records; responds to feedback from auditors*
- *Reviews sources of risk and plans for management of risk*

Responsibility for the Organization's Relationship with its Community

To carry out responsibility for the organization's relationship with its community, a board of directors:

- *Acts as ambassador for the organization to the community*
- *Enhances the organization's public image*
- *Conveys the mission, goals, and achievements to the public*
- *Demonstrates good stewardship of the organization's resources*

Responsibility for the Legal Entity of the Organization
To carry out responsibility for the legal entity of the organization, a board of directors:

- *Ensures conformity to all legal requirements of nonprofit corporate law, the organization's bylaws, and articles of incorporation*
- *Ensures all obligations, such as grants, programs, payroll taxes, etc., are fulfilled*
- *Authorizes up-to-date personnel policies and assures management understanding of those policies*
- *Ensures all employment and income taxes are paid*
- *Reviews and understands financial statements*
- *Ensures that the board itself and its individual members fulfill the legal duties of the board*

The board has many responsibilities. For effective, ethical, and legal operation of the nonprofit it is critical the board knows and understands these responsibilities.

ACTIONS:

Discuss board responsibilities with your fellow board members.

Revise the list above with more responsibilities particular to your board and organization.

The more specific the description of responsibilities, the more likely it is that board members fully understand their obligation to the organization.

CHAPTER 6

INDIVIDUAL MEMBER RESPONSIBILITIES

Every board member has individual duties for which he or she is accountable.

The three legal duties and the board's unified responsibilities are not the only obligations board members must understand and uphold. Every board member has individual duties for which he or she is accountable. Unfortunately, individual member's responsibilities are often misunderstood and overlooked. Board members need to understand, acknowledge, and pledge to fulfill each of the following responsibilities.

Board members are responsible for:

- ***Making a financial contribution to the organization***
  The culture of philanthropy advances every time a board member makes an annual financial donation. The board demonstrates their confidence and credibility when they give. In doing so, they set a great example for the public to follow. Additionally, many funders will not invest in an organization that cannot show 100% contribution rates.

- ***Understanding the organization and its mission***
  A strong organization is comprised of 1 percent vision and 99 percent alignment behind that vision. If the 1 percent is blurred or diluted, the 99 percent becomes mediocre and frustrating.

- ***Getting involved***
  The organization is only as strong as the board. In order to create a sense of full group participation, a board must always be excelling up to a level that is team focused on those it serves. The board must continue to drive in a deep expectation of full participation and engagement from board members. One of the best

things that the board can do is force those that are on it to choose their priorities and reconsider if the board is still one of those top priorities. If it is not, allow them a quick and shameless exit strategy. reconsider if the board is still one of those top priorities. If it is not, allow them a quick and shameless exit strategy.

- ***Avoiding a conflict of interest***
  The board must be able to sustain the interest of the organization, not a personal agenda, at the uppermost in their hearts and minds. Avoiding conflicts of interest dramatically helps board members fulfill their duty of loyalty and build trust.

- ***Attending meetings and required events and being prepared***
  Board meeting attendance is crucial to the board's ability to effectively govern and for the Executive Director to lead. Boards should strive to achieve an average attendance rating of 80 percent. When board members miss meetings, they cannot fulfill the legal governance duties nor can they participate in the board decision-making process. Without learning what is happening within the organization, they are left unable to contribute. Ultimately, it is the individuals that the organization is meant to serve, that end up paying the price for this negligence.

  When a board member misses a meeting, they remain legally responsible for the decisions made in their absence. In other words, absence equals consent to all decisions made in one's absence!

- ***Examining all organizationally relevant materials***
  It is helpful if board members review any materials provided before the meetings. They should strive to maintain this standard as meetings become more focused and engaged in theoretical decision-making governance.

- ***Understanding governing policies, procedures and bylaws***

- ***Taking an active role in fund raising and providing insight into new donor prospects***
  The board is critical in leading the effort of inviting donors to the table to give. Board members will always be more successful than staff at solicitation. Not all board members need to solicit, but the right sub-group should be developed and equipped, including non-board members. This should start with assigning one donor to each board member to simply make contact with, learn why that donor cares, share the vision, learn about them, and what they care about. This will later lead to better ability to meet the needs of that donor and the invitation to give. At least 10 donors per month should be touched (in person, by mail, or by phone to thank them) by the board.

- ***Staying informed on the organization's external environment, the community it serves, and the market in which it operates***

- ***Empowering the Executive Director to lead effectively***
The board is legally charged with evaluating the ED. However, the focus of the evaluation should not be criticism, put rather providing constructive feedback and sharing expectations, two things that will empower the ED to lead more effectively. It is important that the board enjoys a positive peer relationship with the ED.

- ***Supporting peer board members, management, and staff***
The board should maintain a good level of teamwork, camaraderie, and openness. It can use these positive attributes to build even deeper levels of commitment.

  Interpersonal relations facilitate a healthy working environment for the board. When teamwork and personal relationships are weak, trust and openness are also usually weak. It is critical for the board to dig deep into how to forge a true sense of connected passion, vision and team development. Work at finding a way to link board members with a deep personal connection to the cause.

  Interactions among staff and volunteers allow board members to show appreciation and give meaningful feedback. To show appreciation for staff members and volunteers, board members can visit the facility from time-to-time, thank staff through visits and letters, listen to what the staff and volunteers have to say, and show genuine enjoyment of their work.

?

- ***Ensuring a meaningful volunteer experience***
  Members of the board should take care to invest in one another to lead and discover their passion for the cause. If no passion or strong interest resides, provide board members an exit strategy.

- ***Maintaining appropriate boundaries between governance and management of the organization***
  Board members should operate at a framing and leading level rather than getting involved with problem spotting and problem solving.

- ***Showing appreciation to staff and volunteers***
  If board members openly engage staff and volunteers, the board can increase morale and glean important information from the people who work on the frontlines. Board members should appreciate staff contributions to the vision, but understand that it is ultimately the responsibility of the board to cast the vision.

- ***Seeking professional development that will advance your experience and skill as a board member***
  Training equips board members to be successful in carrying out the activities they have committed to performing.

This brief and incomplete list of individual responsibilities illustrates that being a board member requires a commitment of time, energy, and resources. As the old adage goes, boards can only operate as well as their least committed person. If even one individual shirks his or her responsibilities, then the board as a whole will fail to reach its potential of effective leadership.

ACTIONS:

Discuss with your fellow board members the above list of responsibilities.

Make sure that each member understands the responsibilities listed.

Revise and tailor this list to the specific needs of your board and organization. Consider rating each area for the board as a whole.

CHAPTER 7

BOARD SIZE AND STRUCTURE

The ideal board is agile, graceful, responsive and fully present.

Board structure can limit the effectiveness of a board. Overly large boards tend to encourage slow, tedious, and compromised decision-making, while shifting away from meaningful work. They are often overexposed to group dysfunction like "group think," "pluralistic ignorance," and "decision making diffusion." Boards that are too small are limited on collective wisdom and often do not have the resources to provide proper governance and staff a full array of committees and task forces. Boards comprised of twelve to twenty-four members tend to be an ideal size. The ideal board is agile, graceful, responsive and fully present with an understanding of how to use the power entrusted to it.

In addition, boards that do not utilize a working sub-structure tend to lack focus and initiative. A sub-structure can be created through formal committees or ad-hoc task forces and teams. An example of a common sub-structure that tends to foster both characteristics includes the following committees:

- *Executive (situational)*
- *Finance*
- *Strategic Focus and Program Alignment*
- *Board Development: Nominating, Board Leadership Development and Governance*
- *Fund Development and Marketing*
- *Advisory Groups and Special Sub-Teams*

The implementation of a sub-structure begins with the identification of objectives and strategic issues facing the organization in the upcoming twelve to twenty-four months. Each sub-team is to be formed around three to five of the identified objectives and strategic issues. These sub-teams will provide insight into their assigned issues, allowing the full board to stay focused on higher-level issues, such as integrating the mission, vision, and core values.

Board members should be appointed to sub-structure according to their passions and talents. They can be appointed to at least one sub-team, but no more than two. Making appointments in this manner helps the board development team determine if any talent and interest composition gaps exist within the task forces and recruit non-board members to fill the gaps accordingly.

Whenever new objectives and strategic issues arise, and as old ones are accomplished, the task forces or committees can be evaluated to determine whether their strategic focus should be changed and what new task forces should be added or dissolved.

For this process and structure to work effectively, the Executive Director must operate as a peer partner with the board, especially the board chair. The board structure should reflect a connected team of relationships as opposed to a hierarchical structure of superior and subordinated staff relationships. It will be important for the ED to have the capacity to build relationships with board members, and the board chair will need to take time to invest in empowering other board members through connecting with them regularly. Board-centered leadership structure rather than a hierarchical structure requires that the Executive Director and Board Chair invest time in developing other board members to reach their leadership potential.

ACTIONS:

Discuss whether your board is too big or too small.

Does it have a functional committee or task force structure?

Have your members rate your organization as to where it fits on their top 10 most favorite charitable organizations.

Where does it rank? What is the average ranking for your board?

CHAPTER 8

BOARD MEMBER LIABILITY

Nonprofit does not mean "non-liable."

Nonprofit does not mean "non-liable." Certain liabilities originate from the violation of the legal duties of board members or from other areas. In particular, board members can be exposed to the three main liabilities described below.

Liability to the Organization and its Members

Board members are accountable to the organization and its members. The fiduciary obligation to the organization compels board members to act in good faith, loyalty, and in the best interests of the nonprofit organization they are stewarding. Note that this obligation includes, at minimum, board meeting attendance. Regular absences from board meetings may increase a board member's legal liability for decisions made in his or her absence, as absence is considered consent under the law. Violations of this fiduciary obligation, such as being absent from board meetings, could result in negative consequences for the board member. It is important to note, in general, if members act in good faith, loyalty and in the best interest of the nonprofit, a wrong action taken for the right reason is less risky than taking no action.

Statutory Liability

Each board member has the legal duty to be a good steward for the nonprofit by conserving and protecting the assets of the organization and ensuring it is operating within legal and ethical compliance. These responsibilities cannot be abdicated. Violations of this duty could result in legal action against the board or board members.

Liability to Third Parties

Board members are obligated to validate and follow through on contracts with third parties, ensure the contracts are legal, and ensure the contracts do not jeopardize the organization.

In an attempt to protect board members from these liabilities, many nonprofits carry director's and officer's liability insurance. Board members should consider obtaining this insurance if they believe they face a high-risk potential. Although it varies for different organizations, the insurance premium may be purchased by the organization.

In summary, liability should not be ignored, nor should it deter one from sitting on a board.

ACTIONS:

Consult legal counsel on enacting a good director's and officer's liability policy.

Determine if your board is in need of the coverage and if the organization is capable of purchasing the policy.

CHAPTER 9

FINANCIAL MANAGEMENT

Board members should be familiar with six key issues of financial management.

Sound financial management practices are vital for sustaining a healthy nonprofit organization. Whether financial management practices are applied to programs, alternative revenue activities, or contracts, they should not be overlooked. Board members should be familiar with six key issues of financial management.

Issue One: Budgeting

The budget is more than a record of assets and liabilities. It is a living document that indicates the organization's priorities and goals and should be grounded in fulfillment of the mission. A specific committee or task force, such as the finance or budget committee, is usually responsible for the budget's details, but the full board is involved in the budgeting process from the beginning. The full board, not just one committee or task force, is responsible for determining the organization's goals, approving the final version of the budget and evaluating the results.

Issue Two: Fundraising

Board members are responsible for identifying and building revenue sources for the organization, stewarding contributions as well as monitoring the fund development practices. A lack of board involvement in this area can lead to ruin for any nonprofit.

Issue Three: Financial Reporting

The board is responsible for ensuring it receives the necessary financial information to make informed and effective decisions on how to invest in mission fulfillment of the organization. The board should generate financial reporting systems that capture and report the information needed for making these decisions. Failure to do so can result in

inaccurate decisions about fund raising, programs, operating decisions and so forth. The board should consider creating a simple financial dashboard that provides only what is needed to the full board and avoids spending unnecessary time processing through detailed financials as a board team.

Issue Four: The Audit – Understanding Sarbanes-Oxley
Ensure that your board has and utilizes an audit committee and understands the impact of legislation, like the Sarbanes-Oxley Act of 2002. Audits are immensely helpful for the board and are very important for potential funders and donors. The auditor, a certified public accountant, can bring an amazing perspective that has been gained from experience auditing other nonprofit organizations and can identify financial and administrative procedures that need examination or improvement. Consequently, both the audit committee and the full board must learn how to maximize their partnerships with the auditor and find the best way to translate new regulations into practice.

Issue Five: Investments
The board is responsible for defining investment portfolio policies, setting investment guidelines, selecting independent management to handle the investments, and governing the amount of the investment that is available to the operating budget. Usually, it is advisable for the board to create an investment committee to address these issues. In addition, the board should understand the importance of endowment *spending*, not just endowment *saving* and be aware of any real or perceived conflicts of interest.

Issue Six: Accountability

Nonprofit organizations are designed for public service and have been entrusted as stewards of society's resources. As such, nonprofit board members are increasingly being held accountable for their organizations. The board members are responsible for ensuring that practices are ethical, legal, and in the best interest of the organization. A part of this involves making certain that all relevant information is reported on 990s and that no irresponsible or inappropriate actions have occurred.

ACTIONS:

In a board meeting, conduct a board self-evaluation of these areas.

Simply score them, A through F, or 1 to 10 to provide some understanding of where the board is leading well in these areas and where help could be beneficial.

CHAPTER 10

THE DIFFERENCE BETWEEN THE BOARD AND MANAGEMENT

The proper role for the board then is to make sure the organization climbs the right walls.

The distinction between the roles of the board and the roles of management are important but not always well understood. These lines get blurred as both the board and the CEO make strategic leadership and management decisions.

However, the inexact rule that board members lead and managers manage is shaped by:

1. By law, the board, and not management, is ultimately held responsible for the organization.
2. Board members, whether they wish to or not, interfere with management every time they make management decisions. This is not to say that board members should not allow management to make leadership decisions and that board members should never make management decisions. Rather board members should appreciate the spectrum for leading and managing: the less the board leads, the more likely it is to run afoul of its legal duties and obligations. The more the board manages, the more likely it will be to stifle managerial initiative and innovation and limit growth.

The proper role for the board then is to make sure the organization climbs the right walls, and the proper role for management is to climb the walls most efficiently.

The chart below summarizes the responsibilities that accompany each role.

BOARD AND MANAGEMENT: AVOIDING ORGANIZATIONAL DEGRADATION

BOARD:
Making Sure We Are Climbing the Right Wall

- *Upholding Mission*
- *Board Accountability*
- *Counsel to Management*
- *Hire and Fire CEO*
- *Composition & Board Strategy*
- *Long-Term Decision Making*
- *Global Policy*
- *Ambassadorship*
- *Fiduciary Responsibility/Fund Raising*
- *Vision Setting/Holding*
- *Amending the Bylaws*
- *Approving the Budget*
- *Filling Board Vacancies*
- *Enacting Committees/Task Forces*

MANAGEMENT:
Climbing the Wall Most Efficiently

- *Relationship Development*
- *Partner to the Board*
- *Building the Core Organization*
- *Donor Development*
- *Operational Management/ Leadership*
- *Internal/External Assessment*
- *Partnerships*
- *Board Management*
- *Organizational Oversight*
- *Ensuring Strategy/Tactics*

?

ACTIONS:

Discuss the difference between board and management.

Consider adding responsibilities to the previous list that maintain the boundary between counsel and management.

SECTION III

BOARD LEADERSHIP AND CULTURE

CHAPTER 11

GOVERN RESPONSIBLY: BUSINESS-LIKE DOES NOT MEAN BE A BUSINESS

The nonprofit organization is designed to operate in the provision of services that promote the public good.

Nonprofit organizations and the board members who lead them enjoy a distinct relationship with the U.S. economy. Unlike the for-profit sector, the nonprofit sector is bound by a unique dynamic of mission statements, clients, donors, grants, government, non-distribution constraints and so forth.

In the for-profit sector, the financial bottom line can be used as a primary indicator of performance. Measuring performance in the nonprofit sector, on the other hand, is much more subjective because its institutions must first fulfill the stated mission, satisfy the public good and stakeholders, and then subsequently address financial performance.

The nonprofit organization is designed to operate in the provision of services that promote the public good. These areas of need exist because government either cannot meet the need because it is too restrictive or because the for-profit sector cannot provide the service to fill the need due to its inability to generate a profit. Thus, the not-for-profit organization fills the gap and raises the welfare floor by providing a service that others cannot. These favored activities are, by design, areas the organizations typically will operate at a loss for that core service provision, with some exceptions. They are designed to lose money since the service or fee provided is not typically designed to cover the cost of the favored activity.

Some organizations do have models that cover 100 percent of the expense incurred to serve those they seek to benefit, which is commonly seen in healthcare. However, these organizations still must provide charity care to those who cannot pay and often their charitable status is what allows them to maintain a level of quality that a for-profit-organization could not maintain. As we have seen in healthcare, those that can make strong profits are often also being consumed by for-profit organizations. They are often being transitioned into for-profit entities through buy-outs and conversions. In other words, if there is a profit to be made, usually a for-profit will find it and step in. This reality is simply part of our capitalistic system.

As we see, the design of the not-for-profit organization, which is to lose money through its predominant mission-fulfilling activity, is not a bad thing, but rather part of its design and reason for existence. Charitable organizations fill a gap in society, the gap government cannot meet and that for-profits typically cannot make a profit in or do as well with the same quality and trust from society. How much money do we charge a homeless person for his or her night in the shelter? What is the true tuition if a student had to pay their full tuition costs? You get the point.

Due to the fact that most nonprofits operate at a loss, the nonprofit has the need for third party revenues to cover its operating revenue gap. This is covered by contracts, cross subsidization, grants, earned income, endowments, service fees, or philanthropic contributions. This too is part of the design of the not-for-profit organization, making it different from the business or government models of operation. The reliance on community support to deliver a public good is part of the energy and life of a healthy nonprofit organization.

Therefore, board members should not govern and evaluate nonprofit organizations according to limited traditional business indicators like profit and loss alone, nor should they shy away from fundraising and engaging community support. Rather, they should closely examine other performance variables besides profit and loss, such as costs versus societal benefits, mission fulfillment, stewardship of the public good, stakeholder perceptions, donor engagement, and volunteer hours.

However, this does not mean nonprofits cannot utilize sound business principles. They simply need to be aware of the limitations and ramifications of using them, and recognize that some business practices hold value when tailored to fit the nonprofit organization. As a board member, you may be called upon to make decisions that are similar to those facing a business. Remember, the fundamental driving purpose of the nonprofit is the public good, not profit.

CHAPTER 12

BOARD CULTURE, LEADERSHIP, AND GREATNESS

Often, board members understand their duties and obligations, but the board still fails to reach its full potential.

Often, board members understand their duties and obligations, but the board still fails to reach its full potential. One reason for underperformance could be caused by the board's culture, or more precisely, stalemates between different modes of governance that exist within the same board. This also comes from a failure to see the board as the closest donor and volunteer constituency, sitting at the heart of the organization. Keep this in mind as you review the three main kinds of board modes of governance[1] that shape board culture.

Monitor and Police Officer-like Oversight

The board spends most of its time ensuring accountability, overseeing, spotting problems and reviewing details and reports.

Planning, Evaluation, and Strategy

The board spends most of its time finding ways to do the same things better; implementing, evaluating, and adjusting strategy to maximize those impacts.

Discerning and Learning

The board spends most of its time framing the landscape, discerning what is ahead, relating issues and decisions to the mission and vision of the organization, ensuring the right questions are on the table, considering the opportunity costs and how to frame the right strategy.

All three modes are needed to some degree. In the ideal, the board's culture will lean toward focusing 20 percent of its time in Type I leadership, with the rest of the time shifting between Type II and III leadership depending on the situation and its progress.

?

Type III culture dominance is needed to ensure that the board functions as a sense-maker and frames everything, including problem spotting, in accordance to the mission and vision.

A board with a healthy discerning and learning culture focuses intently on:

- ***Getting to the source of underlying issues and framing them within the mission and vision.***
  For example: By performing or ending certain programs, what is the impact on the mission? What are the opportunity costs, in terms of the mission and those programs? Are they equal?

- ***Making sense of the external environment.***
  For example: Do our constituents want, and perhaps strongly expect, for these programs to continue? Do they want the organization to conduct other programs instead? Why is this so?

- ***Weighing the opportunity costs in light of mission and vision.***
  For example: What happens if we eliminate the programs? We may save money, but will we lose our clients and their financial support? In what other ways can we improve revenue and decrease costs without losing our clients' support?

- ***Ensuring decisions and organizational activities fit inside the scope of the mission and vision.***
  For example: Do we advance the mission and vision if we fund certain other programs instead? Can we excel in these programs?

Boards and organizations often struggle to reach greatness, not just because of culture, but because of the inability to focus and operate within so called "high return areas." This means that the board prioritizes its actions according to what it and the organization has passion for, could be or is excellent in, and is able to be sustainable in doing so. In other words, the organization does its best, most valuable work when passion, excellence, and sustainability intersect[2], and the board governs in a thinking, evaluating, and planning mode. It is the job of the board to drive the organization to that point, which is where greatness will be found.

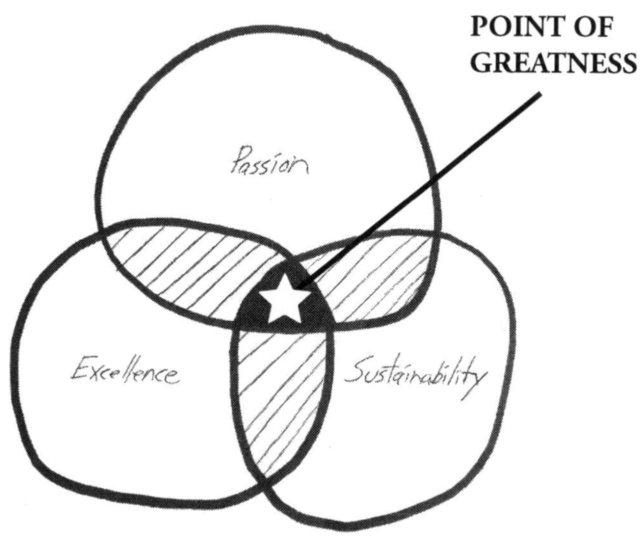

Any priority or organizational activity that falls outside the Point of Greatness will not be as successful nor drive sustainability in the long-term as activities that fit inside the overlapping areas.

The board may find it helpful to understand that its future is driven by two parts:

1. The vision, a future worth aspiring toward
2. Alignment behind the vision.

Clarifying the vision of the organization will be paramount to locating and staying within the boundaries of the Point of Greatness.

Another reason that may prevent a board from reaching its full potential may be the board members' personal agendas. Personal agendas are often adverse to what is in the best interest of the public good and to the organization's mission. This issue should be identified and removed before it causes harm.

A final reason that may prevent a board from reaching its full potential is caused by board member recruitment. Board members may be recruited for a variety of reasons, however, they may not have passion for the organization's cause. Therefore, when the going gets rough, or not fun, or when life gets busy with other charities that are higher up on their favorites list, these board members may not give the organization the full attention it deserves.

Board members recognize the organization as a means for advancing the cause rather than as an end itself. It is important to remember that seeing the organization as a vehicle for the cause helps prevent stagnation and decline.

?

ACTIONS:

Discuss in a board meeting or small group what mode of governance your board spends most of its time, in general and in meetings.

Discuss your organization's higher return areas of points of greatness. Are you in them or outside of them?

Evaluate the board meetings. Are they worth $100 an hour for those who attend? If not, don't meet face to face. Rethink the board agenda based on seeing the board as an asset.

SECTION IV

BOARD MEMBER DEVELOPMENT

CHAPTER 13

INFORMATION MANAGEMENT FOR BOARDS

The board should be kept well-informed, empowered, and well-equipped by the facts.

Critical decisions require accurate, timely, and appropriate information. If the board is to function effectively, it must have the knowledge necessary to make important decisions. The board should be kept well-informed, empowered, and well-equipped by the facts.

To ensure that meetings and information are effective the following guidelines may help:

- *Define the particular facts and statistics needed by members*
- *Define the purpose and agenda for the meeting that limits reports, details and engages members, consider consent agenda*
- *Provide members with periodic and accurate information on budgets, memos, releases, reports, planning documents, policies and procedures and committee reports*
- *Provide as much information in advance as feasible*
- *Open the door for pre-meeting questions or calls*
- *Develop a standard reporting package for members*
- *Provide copies of minutes for review by members*
- *Focus meetings on looking forward as opposed to looking backward*
- *Set a "hard" agenda timeline and stop time*

A primary purpose of good information systems is to effectively and efficiently direct pertinent information to the board members.

ACTIONS:

Use the guidelines above to create an effective, efficient information management system for your board.

Be sure to include the CEO or Executive Director.

CHAPTER 14

NONPROFIT STAKEHOLDER EXPECTATIONS

Ask stakeholders, "How can we, as an organization, better meet YOUR needs?"

Stakeholders—the people impacted by, involved with, or interested in the work of the organization—demand a lot from a nonprofit board. Ironically, most board members do not understand what stakeholders expect of them. It is time well spent to meet with your organization's stakeholders, and discuss their expectations, goals and visions for the organization.

We have learned that stakeholders expect the board to be:

- *Good stewards*
- *Passionate*
- *Mission driven*
- *Approachable*
- *Knowledgeable*
- *Aware of the environment*
- *Accountable Giving*
- *Honest*
- *Ethical*
- *Placing the organization first*
- *Fundraising*
- *Leading by example*
- *Ambassadors for the cause*

One of the most powerful things an organization can do is to ask interested parties, "How can we, as an organization, better meet YOUR needs?"

?

ACTIONS:

Find out the expectations of your stakeholders by inviting them to a board meeting, holding a focus group, or mailing a questionnaire.

Checking in with stakeholders periodically will help the board evaluate their effectiveness and determine if the organization and board are meeting the stakeholder's needs.

CHAPTER 15

MAINTAINING A HEALTHY BOARD

Stagnant boards are missing one common element: passion for the cause.

Keeping a board healthy can be a challenge. Experience indicates that stagnant boards are missing one common element: passion for the cause. A few ideas that may help increase the health of the board are:

Bring passionate, active members on board.
Board members who are passionate about the cause bring unparalleled energy, leadership, and sense of purpose. All of these qualities are essential for productivity.

Board members who are familiar with the organization's mission and purpose are generally able to make better decisions for the organization. Make sure to observe and participate directly in the organization's programs and services so you can truly understand the value of the organization, its connection to the community, and the capabilities of the staff. Also, revisit the organization's mission statement annually to reinforce the organization's purpose.

Attend all meetings.
Being absent from meetings will not necessarily excuse a board member from responsibilities for decisions reached by those in attendance. In fact, absence from meetings increases potential legal liabilities for the board as decisions are made without input from all of its members.

Use sound financial management tools and control systems.
Board members need to learn how to read and use financial statements and audit reports to understand and monitor the organization's fiscal health. Board members also need to understand how their decisions have a financial impact on the organization.

Speak up.

Board members should not remain silent when they disagree with a decision or an opinion expressed by others. Additionally, board members must speak up and ask questions when the organization's goals and objectives are not being met. The board should be a safe place to express any self-perceived inadequacies in understanding responsibilities, as well as a space that provides for and caters to the desire to grow in the appropriate knowledge and skills required to further the organization's needs.

Identify conflicts of interest.

A board member must avoid participating in board discussions or decision-making when there is a conflict of interest. Even the perception of a conflict of interest must be avoided, if possible. If faced with an actual or perceived conflict, board members must inform the other directors of the situation and excuse themselves from related areas of decision-making and transactions.

Establish personnel policies.

In addition to having personnel policy guidelines for the Chief Executive Officer or Executive Director, the board must be certain the organization's personnel policies are adequate and updated to reflect all applicable laws.

Develop personal plans of involvement.

Develop individual plans of expectations for each member.

Set up renewal retreats.

Define times during the year to get board members focused on the mission, impact, and importance of their service.

Connect members socially.
Ensure members connect at a social level, share things outside of board service, and are comfortable with one another as partners.

View current and past members of the board as long-term relationships.
The board must remember that fellow board members represent the organization's closest constituent group, those who not only govern the organization but also serve on its behalf. Emphasis should be placed on developing long-term relationships with board members, both during and after their board tenure.

To ensure its continued health, a board should:

- *Evaluate members every two to three years*
- *Evaluate individual members every one to two years*
- *Conduct retreats to build cohesion and enthusiasm*
- *Assess the needs of the individual members yearly*
- *Define plans to keep board members fulfilled*
- *Build ownership in the organization*
- *Periodically define and re-define the board's values*
- *Seek out additional board training and education*
- *Seek to understand how the board needs to evolve*
- *Find out how members are doing and what they need*

ACTIONS:

Develop a plan for maintaining individual and whole board productivity.

Construct board member evaluations and whole board evaluations, including criteria and time frame for performance review.

Seek outside consultant to help with board evaluation if necessary.

SECTION V

BOARD MEMBER RECRUITMENT AND COMPOSITION

CHAPTER 16

WHY WOULD SOMEONE WANT TO SERVE ON A BOARD?

A primary purpose for serving as a board member is a strong shared passion for the common cause.

Each person has his or her reasons for voluntary board service. Volunteering as a board member is an honor that should not be taken lightly. Understanding the different motivations of board members can help the board address the needs of its members and foster internal cohesion. Often, the motivation that leads to the most cohesiveness, commitment, and care is a firm belief in the organization's cause and mission. Ideally, a primary purpose for serving as a board member is a strong shared passion for the common cause.

A CLOSER LOOK

A snap shot of the average US board, taken from BoardSource[1]:

- *Average board has 15.3 members*
- *Average board Term is 3.1 years*
- *Average board has 5.4 committees*
- *Average board members serve 2.4 consecutive terms*
- *74% of boards have a structured orientation program*
- *Nationally, 56% of boards have 100% giving rates, with an average rate of 86%*
- *Average board meets 7.3 times per year*
- *Average board meeting lasts 3.3 hours*
- *Nationally, 88% of boards have a board attendance rate of 75% or higher*

CHAPTER 17

WHAT TO LOOK FOR IN A GOOD BOARD MEMBER

The number one thing to look for is passion, interest, and shared value with the organization's mission.

Knowing what to look for in a prospective board member can be difficult. Use the following list of characteristics as a guide when looking for new board members.

Passion.
The number one thing to look for is passion, interest, and shared value with the organization's mission.

Abilities.
Seek people with varying abilities from visioning the future, being creative, listening, ability to analyze, ability to work with others, think clearly, problem-solve, resolve conflicts, learn, and build relationships.

Personal qualities.
Seek someone with commitment, the ability to fully participate, enthusiasm, honesty, integrity, values, a sense of humor, a willing spirit, a generous heart, passion for the cause, an understanding of the need for reflection, and sensitivity.

Interests.
Seek someone with willingness to learn and develop skills that they may need. Candidates should also be willing to work, network, and think outside of the norm.

Integrity.
Board members must be persons of high integrity. On a board, any appearance of improper dealings is completely unacceptable. Any conflict of interest, actual or perceived, is troublesome in deliberations, and is potentially damaging to the organization.

The best board members bring to the table neither their personal prejudices nor their own agendas. They are people of integrity and courage. They come with a broad perspective and a willingness to search out solutions. They know that the problems they will face are complex and the solutions are not simple. They are comfortable making tough decisions, even if the correct choice is the least flawed of several imperfect options.

Competence.
Board members are often recruited for their expertise in a certain area. Their expertise may include areas of legal, financial, technological, religious, leadership, and so forth. Even when board members are not recruited for a specific expertise, they should still be chosen for their principles, interests, and personal qualities.

Personality Types on the Board.
If you research board member personality types, you will find some humorous but real descriptions. A few of these descriptions include the following:

- *The "Johnny-one-note," who is obsessed with a single issue*
- *The devil's advocate, who persists in taking the contrary view just for show*
- *The authority figure, accustomed to commanding and uncomfortable with group decisions*
- *The "off-the-wall-artist," a self-centered individual who raises problems in order to give speeches on them, who has an opinion on everything but seldom has done his homework*
- *The "board hopper" who sits on many boards but serves none*

ACTIONS:

Develop a list of qualities and characteristics to seek in potential new board members.

When doing this, consider the current composition of your board.

Do you have adequate diversity of gender, race, background, skills, and abilities to adequately reflect the community you serve and provide the best leadership?

SECTION VI

BOARD AND FUNDRAISING: PHILANTHROPIC SUSTAINABILITY

CHAPTER 18

CREATING SUSTAINABILITY: FUNDRAISING AND THE BOARD

Every time a board member makes financial donation, they demonstrate their confidence and credibility in the organization.

The board's obligation to participate in fund development stems from the responsibilities it has to the organization, the organization's financial performance, and the greater community. Participation in the fund development program comes in two forms.

First, every board member should make a meaningful annual financial gift to the organization according to his or her means. By doing so, board members indicate to the donors and the community they stand behind the organization. In other words, the simple action of giving establishes credible authority. It sends a message of stability and care; opening the door to many donors, foundations, and corporations who will not support an organization that cannot show a 100 percent board contribution rate. It is not about how much board members give but rather whether they give at all. Board member contributions and the trust they establish, are critical in this era where the nonprofit sector constantly struggles with issues of trust and accountability.

A commonly heard comment made by donors is, "If their whole board cannot even give a dollar, why would I give to their organization? Why do they believe I should give or give more?"

Every time a board member makes a voluntary annual financial donation, they demonstrate their confidence and credibility in the organization and advance the culture of philanthropy. This serves as a great example for the community to follow. That is why many nonprofit organizations strive for a 100 percent board member contribution rate with a focus of making meaningful donations and not the bottom line dollar amount.

Second, every board member should participate in the donor development and fundraising process. Board members should act as ambassadors for the organization, establish relationships with existing and potential donors, and solicit donations. Not every board member has to solicit donations —some board members may be more comfortable and have greater ability in this area than others. Rather, all board members should be assigned a fundraising task, whether it is stuffing envelopes, writing thank you letters, giving thanks over the phone, or visiting donors in person.

Board members have the most fundraising success when they understand philanthropy. Specifically, how true fundraising is focused on the donor's relationship, not simply his or her checkbook, to the organization. Sustainable fundraising is relationship-focused and based on an exchange of values with potential and existing donors.

Rather than seeing donors as commodities or a check book, the healthy organization should see the donor as someone who will be giving in twenty years and value the donors for their relationship to and advocacy for the cause; not just for their gift. Donors make token gifts to organizations that view them as checkbooks or commodities, but they make sacrificial and planned gifts to organizations that view them as close relationships, even as family.

Board members should create personal relationships with these donors and seek to strengthen the links that bind the donor to the organization, turning donors into advocates for the organization and the cause. They should allow the donors to get involved with strategy and planning, within bounds. Above all, board members should take the time to listen to the donors' needs and expectations, which might simply occur over a cup of coffee.

Serving as an ambassador means much more than attending board meetings and the occasional fundraising event; it involves spending time in the community and having conversations about the organization and the cause. It involves building meaningful relationships and strong bonds with constituents, seeking to serve donors and actively seeking their philanthropic support and setting an example by making financial contributions. Ultimately, it involves establishing a culture of philanthropy that is both mission and donor-focused and sees the volunteer and the donor as life-time relationships that should be invested in.

Key responsibilities for board members include:

- ***Placing a high priority on fundraising:***
  Fundraising needs to be placed as a top priority. It is the board's job to ensure the organization devotes enough resources for fundraising activities, setting the tone for the culture of philanthropy in the organization.

- ***Participating in the fund development program:***
  Board member participation is a vital component of a successful fund development program. It gives the program credibility, as many donors will want to speak and confer with those who lead and govern the organization.

- ***Using the Personal Plan of Involvement:***
  Board members should be assigned activities they are interested in. Board member participation dramatically increases the number of people who can carry out cultivation, stewardship, and solicitation activities.

- ***Advancing the culture of philanthropy:***
  Each board member has the ability to further their own calling while transforming the world around them through making voluntary and personal contributions.

- ***Viewing fundraising as a long-term investment:***
  Boards that view fundraising as a long-term investment rather than a quick fix are much more likely to build enduring fundraising programs, instill a culture of philanthropy, and create long-term relationships with donors.

- ***Serving as ambassadors:***
  This activity is a key component for developing community relationships and enlarging the donor base. Most board members should seek to serve as ambassadors and publicly represent the organization.

- ***Listening to donors:***
  This is a fundamental element of donor cultivation. Without it, donor relationships rarely progress long-term. Board members should desire to be out with donors in one-on-one settings listening and gathering insights. This can be as easy as discussing the latest organizational news and plans over a cup of coffee.

- ***Thanking donors:***
  This activity is a fundamental element of donor stewardship. Donors need to be thanked in a meaningful manner in order to feel recognized and appreciated. The board's role is to personally thank as many donors as possible, beginning with the largest donors. Donor stewardship must be a priority for all members, not just those few to whom gracious appreciation comes naturally.

- ***Fundraising training:***
  Fundraising training equips board members to be successful in carrying out the fundraising activities they have committed to performing. Secure adequate fundraising training for each and every board member; do not risk having uninformed, unprepared members. Prepare a program to hold appropriate techniques and lessons on how to fundraise. Do not assume members already have the knowledge or will attain it on their own. Remove any embarrassment by making training accessible for all levels of knowledge. Allow room for ignorance to be obliterated through honest dialogue amongst members.

- ***Personal Solicitation:***
  The board is critical in leading the effort of inviting donors to the table to give. Board members will always be more successful than staff at solicitation. Not all board members need to solicit, but the right sub-group should be developed and equipped, including non-board members. This should start with assigning one donor to each board member to simply make contact with, learn why that donor cares, share the

vision, learn about them, and what they care about. This will later lead to better ability to meet the needs of that donor and the invitation to give. At least 10 donors per month should be contacted, in person, by mail, or by phone, to have them thanked by the board.

In addition, board members should adopt and follow a Donor Bill of Rights, such as the one developed by the American Association of Fundraising Counsel on the next page.

ACTIONS:

At your next board meeting, discuss and decide on what you believe your culture of fundraising to be.

Is the donor a checkbook or a long-term relationship?

Strive to reach a 100% board contribution rate. Adopt a Donor Bill of Rights.

A DONOR BILL OF RIGHTS:

Philanthropy is based on voluntary action for the common good. It is a tradition of giving and sharing that is primary to the quality of life. To assure that philanthropy merits the respect and trust of the general public, and that donors and prospective donors can have full confidence in the not-for-profit organizations and causes they are asked to support, we declare that all donors have these rights:

1. *To be informed of the organization's mission, of the way the organization intends to use donated resources, and of its capacity to use donations effectively for their intended purposes.*

2. *To be informed of the identity of those serving on the organization's governing board, and to expect the board to exercise prudent judgment in its stewardship responsibilities.*

3. *To have access to the organization's most recent financial statements.*

4. *To be assured their gifts will be used for the purposes for which they were given.*

5. *To receive appropriate acknowledgement and recognition.*

6. *To be assured that information about their donations is handled with respect and with confidentiality to the extent provided by law.*

7. To expect that all relationships with individuals representing organizations of interest to the donor will be professional in nature.

8. To be informed whether those seeking donations are volunteers or employees of the organization.

9. To have the opportunity for their names to be deleted from mailing lists that an organization may intend to share.

10. To feel free to ask questions when making a donation and to receive prompt, truthful, and forthright answers.

Developed by: American Association of Fundraising Counsel (AAFRC), Association for Healthcare Philanthropy (AAHP), Council for Advancement and Support of Education (CASE), Association of Fundraising Professionals (AFP). Initial endorsers: Independent Sector, National Catholic Development Conference (NCDC), National Committee on Planned Giving (NCPG), National Council for Resource Development (NCRD), United Way of America[1].

CHAPTER 19

A CHECKLIST FOR BUILDING AN EFFECTIVE BOARD

Work to ensure your board will fulfill its purpose and lead a successful and sustainable organization.

Review the following list of characteristics of effective boards. As you build or remodel your board, use this checklist to ensure your board will fulfill its purpose and lead a successful and sustainable organization.

An effective board will:
Include members with the needed skills, experiences, and abilities to help the organization realize its mission.

Ensure your board:

- *Establishes and follows a process to identify board skills to help meet goals within the strategic plan*
- *Recruits new board members who fill in a need or a gap with skills, experiences, or abilities*

An effective board will:
Set criteria for board member recruitment and institute a strategy.

Ensure your board:

- *Establishes and follows a recruitment process with clear evaluative criteria*
- *Ensures a continuous recruitment process that looks to a wide range of sources and to the future*

An effective board will:
Strive for diversity.

Ensure your board:

- *Discusses and understands the value of diversity; determines the types of diversity needed to accurately reflect the community you serve*
- *Plans for diversity when recruiting new board members*

An effective board will:
Set term limits.

Ensure your board:

- *Understands that term limits enable a board to bring in new members/skills*
- *Retains valuable directors by providing means for them to stay involved*

An effective board will:
Orient new members.

Ensure your board:

- *Designs/delivers formal orientation on mission, structure, finances, responsibilities, committees, fundraising, etc.*

?

An effective board will:
Utilize an effective process for determining board leadership.

Ensure your board:
- *Agrees on a process to select strong leadership for the board/committees*
- *Sets term limits for leadership*

An effective board will:
Encourage and develop board leaders.

Ensure your board:
- *Rotates committee assignments to allow board members to develop leadership skills and experience*
- *Develops a plan to ensure continuous, effective leadership*

An effective board will:
Have effective leaders.

Ensure your board:
- *Empowers directors who have the necessary skills, enthusiasm, energy, and time to become leaders*
- *Ensures members make meaningful contributions*

An effective board will:
Arrive prepared for meetings.

Ensure your board:
- *Sets meeting dates for the year*
- *Distributes meeting agendas, including areas of focus and background material, to attendees prior to meetings*

An effective board will:
Hold effective meetings.

Ensure your board:
- *Starts and ends meetings on time*
- *Manages time to ensure adequate board discussion on important topics*
- *Encourages board member contribution and participation*

An effective board will:
Enjoy being a board.

Ensure your board:
- *Exhibits fun and passion for the organization and its work*
- *Connects to the organization's mission*

INDEX

Chapter 1: Philanthropy and the Board

1. "Quick Facts About Nonprofits." *Quick Facts About Nonprofits | NCCS*, nccs.urban.org/data-statistics/quick-facts-about-nonprofits.

2. "Your Guide To Intelligent Giving." *Charity Navigator*, www.charitynavigator.org/index.cfm?bay=content.view.

3. Brice McKeever and Marcus Gaddy. "The Nonprofit Workforce: By the Numbers." *Non Profit News | Nonprofit Quarterly*, 13 Jan. 2017, nonprofitquarterly.org/2016/10/24/nonprofit-workforce-numbers/.

4. "The Value of Volunteer Time." *Independent Sector*, independentsector.org/resource/the-value-of-volunteer-time/.

Chapter 2: The Nonprofit Board Today

1, 2, 3. Internal Revenue Service, 2013

Chapter 12: Board Culture, Leadership, and Greatness

1. Chait, Ryan, Taylor. *Governance as Leadership.* John Wiley & Sons, Inc., Hoboken, New Jersey, 2005.

2. Collins, Jim. *Good to Great.* HarperCollins Publishers Inc., New York, NY, 2001.

Chapter 16: Why Would Someone Want to Serve on a Board?

1. "Leading With Intent: 2017 National Index of Nonprofit Board Practices" *Leading With Intent | BOARDSOURCE*, https://leadingwithintent.org/

Chapter 18: Creating Sustainability: Fundraising and the Board

1. "Donor Bill of Rights." American Association of Fundraising Counsel, 1993.

ABOUT THE AUTHOR

Jamie D. Levy is the President and Chief Vision Officer of JDLevy & Associates and founding partner of FiscAlign accounting and financial services and Discover Philanthropy. Jamie is also a faculty member at Indiana University, where he teaches in the graduate and professional programs in not-for-profit management and development. Through his teaching and consulting, he has trained tens of thousands of professionals from some 30 countries. He has become recognized as an international expert in the area of nonprofit organizational development and social impact. He is an officially designated U.S. Department of Labor nonprofit industry field expert and is appointed to the Indiana University O'Neill School of Public and Environmental Affairs Distinguished Alumni Council.

JDLevy & Associates' services focus on four key areas:

- *Vision*
- *Culture*
- *Impact*
- *Sustainability*

Learn more at jdlevyassociates.com.

Made in the USA
Columbia, SC
03 August 2024

39553358R00088